A souvenir guide

# Giant's Causeway
## County Antrim

Anna Groves

United Nations
Educational, Scientific and
Cultural Organization

World Heritage
in the United Kingdom

Fathoming a Fabled Landscape   2

3

4

6

8

10

12

Transferred for safekeeping   14

Looking to the future   16

The Cause of Much Inspiration   18

The story of Finn McCool   19

The origin of Finn   20

A long-lost love story   21

The Causeway's reputation grows   22

Garrulous guides   24

The Giant's Causeway Coast   centrefold

Sightseeing from the sea   26

A booming trade   28

The art of the Causeway   30

The Causeway Today   32

Portnaboe   34

Port Ganny   35

The Little Causeway   36

The Middle Causeway   37

The Grand Causeway   38

Port Noffer   40

Port na Spaniagh   42

In the seas   44

In the skies   46

Beneath our feet   47

Nature has the last word   48

Front cover A golden light falls on the honeycomb of the Grand Causeway

Inside front cover Anyone home? A walker looks down on the Giant's Chimneys

Left The Giant's Boot in Port Noffer

Back cover These onion skin formations are just one of many fascinating features found along the Giant's Causeway Coast

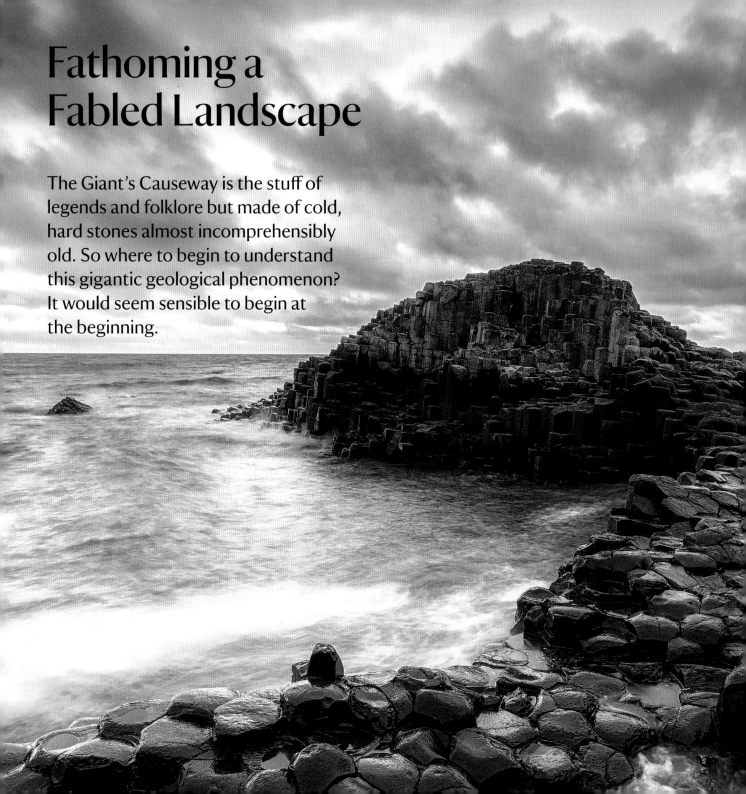

# Fathoming a Fabled Landscape

The Giant's Causeway is the stuff of legends and folklore but made of cold, hard stones almost incomprehensibly old. So where to begin to understand this gigantic geological phenomenon? It would seem sensible to begin at the beginning.

# The origins of
# the Causeway

'It looks like the beginning of the world, somehow: the sea looks older than in other places, the hills and rocks strange, and formed differently from other rocks and hills – as those vast dubious monsters were formed who possessed the earth before man.... When the world was moulded and fashioned out of a formless chaos, this must have been the bit over – a remnant of chaos!' So wrote the author W. M. Thackeray when he visited the Giant's Causeway in 1842. That was nearly 200 years ago and over 100 years after the Causeway came to public attention.

Primeval it may appear, but we don't have to go quite as far back as the origins of history to explain this remarkable formation. The story of the Causeway begins 60 million years ago, when the supercontinent known as Pangaea was dividing to create the Atlantic Ocean between what would become the Americas and Europe.

## An ever-changing world

The landmass of Pangaea, as the Earth's lands do today, rested on tectonic plates. These, and there are seven or eight of them depending on how they are defined, make up the rigid outermost shell of our planet. They are in constant motion as they glide over the mantle, a viscous, hot layer of magma (molten rock) and other semi-solid rocks and minerals. When the plates move apart or against one another, seismic events such as earthquakes and eruptions occur, creating mountains and fissures, shaping the world we see today. The Causeway is one of the more dramatic manifestations of the Earth's power.

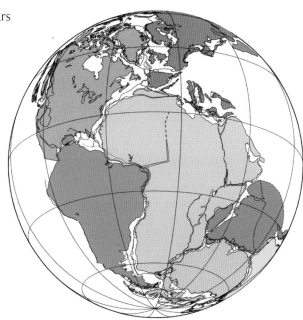

Left The Causeway, exposed by the action of glaciers and lashed by waves ever since, is a dynamic and dramatic place

Right Pangaea 200 million years ago, before Eurasia and Africa separated from the Americas to open up the Atlantic Ocean

# The power of the landscape

**Dramatic the formation of the Causeway may have been, but it didn't happen all at once. Aeons and Ice Ages passed. Earth, fire, water and air, all the elemental forces combined to create the now familiar but fascinating landscape of the Causeway.**

When Pangaea divided to form the Atlantic Ocean, lava escaped through fissures and poured out in a series of eruptions, thousands of years apart, over many millions of years. These lava flows spread across much of today's County Antrim and the Scottish islands. When the lava cooled it formed what we call basalt, and over time a large plateau of basalt rocks built up, stretching all the way from Cave Hill overlooking Belfast to Binevenagh, a mountain in County Derry~Londonderry.

## A change in the weather

We're all familiar with the concept of climate change, but the Earth's climate has been through many dramatic changes, one of which is thought to have caused the mass extinction of the dinosaurs at the end of the Cretaceous period, around 66 million years ago. Following this was the Palaeocene period – the beginning of the 'age of mammals' – with a warming climate and

Above A thick layer of laterite in the cliffs to the west of the Giant's Causeway

intense rainfall that broke down the top layer of that basalt rock we mentioned earlier. Over hundreds of thousands of years, this created a thick layer of red soil, called laterite, which was in turn eroded in places to form river valleys. You can see this red layer today, up to 15 metres (49 feet) thick, in some of the cliffs at the Causeway; it's like the 'jam' in a giant basalt sandwich.

## A cool transformation

So where did the next layer of basalt come from? Another dramatic change and a new flow of lava, much bigger and thicker than those that went before. Up to 100 metres (330 feet) thick in places, it filled up a river valley and slowly began to cool.

It is at this cooling process that things start to get really interesting. At the bottom of the deep pool, regular cracks formed where the lava rested against the existing, cooler, material below. Cracks started at points, and then each spread out in three prongs, roughly 120 degrees apart. As the cracks lengthened they met other cracks and formed polygonal shapes: think of the shapes you see in cooling mud. As the whole pool cooled and the lava contracted, the cracks moved up from the base of the flow and, due to the very regular consistency and chemistry of the lava, they created columns.

Whereas the lava at the bottom of the pool cooled slowly, nearer the surface the lava cooled in contact with the air and surface water, forming uneven rocks and blocks rather than columns.

Right The polygonal shapes of the Causeway columns were formed in a process similar to when mud cools and cracks

Above right The soaring and uncannily regular columns of the Giant's Organ

## Carving out the Causeway

This process was repeated over the next 40 million years, with further eruptions and formations of basalt layers, until the next big climatic change: the last Ice Age. About three million years ago, the spread of ice sheets in the Northern Hemisphere began. Where the Giant's Causeway now stands, a mighty glacier advanced across the landscape, weighing down the land and scraping at the rocks and soils. When the ice retreated from the area, maybe a million years later, the columns of the Causeway were finally revealed.

Now exposed to the effects of wind and wave, the coastline of the Causeway changed again as bays and headlands were formed. Pounded by the wild North Atlantic Ocean, the top of the flow was gradually removed, leaving some of the regular columns from the bottom of the ancient lava pool behind.

So you see, the Giant's Causeway is the product of a dynamic planet and its forces, formed over millions of years and still changing.

# Other causeways

The Giant's Causeway (X) is arguably the most famous collection of rock columns, but there are other, even larger formations. More than resembling the columns of the Giant's Causeway, the formations described below were also formed during the opening up of the North Atlantic Ocean.

### Doon Point, Rathlin Island, Northern Ireland

These columns are the Causeway's closest relation, formed a while before the Causeway columns but from the same sequence of eruptions that helped create the Causeway. The island is composed of black basalt sitting on a bed of white chalk; it was described by Charles Kingsley in *Westward Ho* (1855) as a 'drowned Magpie'.

### Fingal's Cave, Island of Staffa, Scotland

Fingal's Cave is named after the Scottish equivalent of the Causeway giant – Fionn mac Cumhaill – proof surely of the fabled bridge that once extended across the sea? Staffa and the cave are now part of a National Nature Reserve looked after by the National Trust for Scotland.

### The Faroe Islands

Lying halfway between Scotland and Iceland, these islands owe their existence to a series of lava eruptions, just like those that occurred at the Causeway. The whole sequence of Faroese lava flows built up to a depth of nearly 3,000 metres (nearly 2 miles). Columns are mostly found towards the top of the lower set of 40 to 50 flows.

## Susanna Drury

Edwin Sandys' drawings were instrumental in helping Molyneux draw his conclusions, but the first trustworthy views of the Giant's Causeway were by an obscure but very able painter named Susanna Drury. Her birth and death dates are not known, but she was the sister of a Dublin miniature painter called Franklin, who died in 1771.

Her paintings, two pairs of pictures, each with an 'East' and a 'West Prospect', won a competition held by the Dublin Society (the Irish equivalent of the Royal Society of Arts).

As well as prize money of £25, she won acclaim and many admirers who copied her work. One copy was included in the *Encyclopédie, ou dictionnaire raisonné des sciences, des arts et des métiers*, published in France between 1751 and 1772, and one of the key texts of the European Enlightenment.

More than being lovely to look at, Susanna's accurate paintings allowed scientists to develop new theories about the Causeway, feeding into the debate raging around the origin of rocks between 'Neptunists' and 'Vulcanists'.

Above Thomas Molyneux was the first scholar to make a serious study of the Causeway

Left Edwin Sandys' drawing of the Giant's Causeway including a detailed study of ball-and-socket joints (top right)

Right Susanna Drury's paintings of the east (top) and west (bottom) prospects

# Early debates

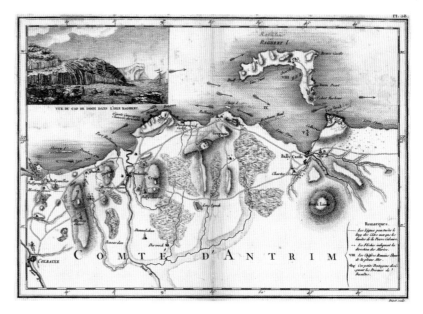

As word of the Causeway spread and more scientists speculated about its origins, naturally theories abounded. At first the Causeway raised more questions than it answered about the formation of the Earth, dividing strongly held opinions.

The Causeway came under 'scientific' scrutiny in the 1740s, during the Age of Enlightenment (1620s–1780s). This was an era in which cultural and intellectual forces in Western Europe emphasised reason, analysis and individualism rather than traditional lines of authority, that is to say, the Church. The first scientists to study the Causeway naturally dismissed tales of giants as superstitious nonsense, but their own studies were in their infancies. Geological science had not yet been established, and academic study was confined to gentlemen's libraries rather than carried out in the field.

But that didn't stop them formulating some interesting and sometimes opposing theories. One of the more intriguing disputes arose between those who believed the columns came from under the Earth's surface and those who believed they were formed underwater.

## Fire versus water

The Vulcanists believed the former (Vulcan was the Roman god of fire), the Neptunists the latter (Neptune being the Roman god of the sea). Thomas Molyneux had concluded that the columns were made of basalt, but he didn't know that basalt was formed from lava. In 1763 a Frenchman, Nicolas Desmarest, travelled to observe basalt columns in the Auvergne region of France. Thanks to Susanna Drury's engravings, Desmarest was well aware of the Giant's Causeway. He compared the French columns to the Causeway when he contributed to the Encyclopédie; a subsequent edition contains engravings of the French columns next to a copy of the Drury pictures. In 1774 Desmarest published his theory that basalt came from lava and he was subsequently dubbed the founder of Vulcanism.

Left Nicolas Desmarest, who was the first to suggest that the Causeway was the result of volcanic activity

Above A map of County Antrim by Nicolas Desmarest published 1827; Doon Point on Rathlin Island is inset top left

This theory was challenged by a German scientist called Abraham Gottlob Werner, who believed all rocks had formed out of a great original ocean, through a process called sedimentation. He cited the lack of a lava source as the problem with the Vulcanist theory; this discussion was before tectonic plates were known about and the possibility of lava erupting from fissures as well as volcanoes. Indeed, Desmarest had mistaken the steep headland on one of Susanna Drury's paintings for a volcano.

## An age-old debate

As the scientists pored over their rock samples and made their various observations, an idea emerged that was troubling to some. At that time the commonly held belief about the Earth's creation was the version laid out in the Bible. However, in 1785 James Hutton, the founder of modern geology, was developing his theories about rock formation and finding that the processes involved happened incredibly slowly, therefore the Earth must be much older than previously supposed. He also argued that basalt was once molten (so not formed in the oceans as the Neptunists believed) and the heat source was in the planet's core.

## Agreement at last

Over the next 200 years, the debates continued, but today scientists are agreed that the heat of the Earth was the driving force behind the formation of the Giant's Causeway and the evidence points to volcanic events arising around 60 million years ago.

Left James Hutton, the founder of modern geology; by Henry Raeburn

# Building on interest

**Stones may have been removed for study and as souvenirs, but the interest the Causeway drew from academics and from tourists meant that significant structures were built as well as taken away.**

When people first started coming to the Giant's Causeway (and it was not only scientists but also tourists, as the fashionably dressed women in Susanna Drury's paintings attest) the journey was long and arduous with the nearest lodgings in Bushmills just over two miles away. So in 1836 an enterprising local woman, Miss Elizabeth Henry, leased a four-acre field from the Macnaghtens, and established an inn, the Causeway Hotel. She built the main part of the hotel we still know today in 1841, to the highest standards. Sadly she died within a few years of its completion.

But the Causeway Hotel, for all its refinement, was not without its competitors. There was a keen rivalry between the Causeway Hotel and the nearby Kane's Refreshment Rooms built on the family farmstead. Kane's was rebuilt in the late 1870s with 'sleeping apartments' and renamed Kane's Royal Hotel, thanks to proprietor Mary Jane Kane, who pounced on the Prince of Wales' party during his visit to the Causeway in 1876, and had him in for tea!

Top The Causeway Hotel in the 1880s or 1890s with the ornate wooden teahouse in its grounds

Left The formidable Mary Jane Kane

## The coming of the railway

In 1887, the lease of the Causeway Hotel was taken over by the Traill brothers, founders of the Causeway tram. The world's first hydroelectric tram, it was powered by the River Bush with the plant at Walkmill Falls. Their initial idea was to use the tram to transport sand, gravel, salmon, iron ore and agricultural produce, but seeing that visitors to the Causeway used the tram to get as far as Bushmills, they extended the line in 1887 and built a tram station conveniently close to the hotel they'd just acquired. It featured a pretty little waiting room, nicknamed 'the Pagoda', which was specially bought from Switzerland at a cost of £400.

## Guides at war

Competition between the guides was already fierce, but business got cut-throat when the Causeway tram started running in 1887. Its terminus was in the grounds of the Causeway Hotel and soon it was bringing tens of thousands of visitors each year, met by guides engaged by the Traills. This led to a 'war' between guides attached to the Causeway Hotel and the rest of the guides. There were frequent squabbles and even occasional fistfights – all part of the entertainment!

Happily the 'guide war' ended in 1910, when Francis Kane bought the Causeway Hotel, bringing the two hotels under the same ownership and allowing the guides to divide custom more harmoniously between themselves. Francis added the name of Kane to the outside of the hotel and painted it a striking red. He also removed the ornate teahouse that used to stand in the grounds.

## Post-war tourism

The 1920s and 1930s were golden years for the Giant's Causeway, and the hotels and the tram did brisk business. But the rise of road transport started to take its toll on numbers using the tram. During the Second World War there was a huge boost to the tram, as soldiers needed to be transported to and from a large army camp established near the Causeway. But after the war, visitor numbers could not recover in time to prevent it from closing. In 1999, 50 years after that last service, the Giant's Causeway and Bushmills Railway Company re-laid a track between Bushmills and the Causeway, and began operating a steam locomotive on a narrow gauge railway, giving something of a flavour of what it was like to travel to the Causeway by tram.

Business for the hotels similarly dwindled and Kane's Royal Hotel had stopped taking guests long before it was finally demolished in 1963. However, the Causeway Hotel as we know it today stayed in business, still run by the Kane family, until it was bought by the National Trust in 2001. Refurbished in 2011–12, today it provides a warm welcome to a whole new generation of visitors, 170 years after its first guests.

Above The Causeway Hotel tram stop with its Pagoda waiting room

Right The proprietor of both hotels, Francis Kane and his wife Kate

# Transferred for safekeeping

**The National Trust has cared for the Giant's Causeway for over 50 years. In that time it has been recognised as one of Northern Ireland's most precious landscapes, and it is the Trust's task to protect it whilst giving the public access to this remarkable place.**

In 1961 the National Trust acquired the Giant's Causeway – with support from the Ulster Land Fund, together with a gift of land from Sir Anthony Macnaghten – and opened the Causeway to the public the following year. Two years later, the Trust opened the first 10 miles of the North Antrim Coastal Path. Today, just one aspect of the Trust's work is maintaining the extensive network of trails, giving visitors access to stunning views of the spectacular coastline and countryside of the Causeway. There are approximately six miles of trails within the Giant's Causeway site, with another four miles running all the way to Carrick-a-Rede.

## Worldwide recognition

In 1986, 25 years after the National Trust took over caring for the site, the Giant's Causeway was designated as a World Heritage Site (WHS). For this to happen, a place must be nominated by a country's government to the United Nations Educational, Scientific and Cultural Organisation (UNESCO). They consider the site and if it is deemed to have 'outstanding universal value', then it is 'inscribed' onto the World Heritage List. There are three types of World Heritage Site – natural, cultural and mixed (both natural and cultural). The Giant's Causeway is a natural World Heritage Site, not only for the amazing beauty of its landscape but also because of what it shows us about the Earth's ancient past.

## Precious and protected

This designation by UNESCO conferred the highest status on the Giant's Causeway, but this spectacular landscape has been repeatedly singled out for recognition. In 1987 the Causeway slopes and headlands were designated as a National Nature Reserve (NNR). This is because the geology and resulting shape of the Causeway bays have created an amazing range of habitats (see pages 44–47).

Then in 1989 the area around the Giant's Causeway was recognised as an Area of Outstanding Natural Beauty (AONB). AONBs are landscapes of 'particularly distinctive character, remarkable natural beauty and high ecological value'.

In the year 2000 the Causeway and surrounding landscape received further recognition in international law, when it became the North Antrim Coast Special Area of Conservation. Nationally it was recognised as an Area of Special Scientific Interest (ASSI) in the same year.

## Continuing care

The significance and protection of the Giant's Causeway are enshrined in international and national law. All these designations – WHS, NNR, AONB, ASSI – make official what the millions who have visited the Causeway have discovered for themselves: the uniqueness of the landscape, the breathtaking scenery, the wild and unspoilt nature of the place. It's no small task, but all the Causeway's staff and volunteers, together with the help of local landowners and farmers, work with equal measures of pride and passion to keep this place special and open for all to enjoy.

'What makes the concept of World Heritage exceptional is its universal application. World Heritage sites belong to all the peoples of the world, irrespective of the territory on which they are located.'

UNESCO

# Looking to the future

**The single biggest change to the site of the Giant's Causeway in recent years is the striking yet sympathetically designed visitor centre, which opened in July 2012. It is confidently modern while providing a gateway to this prehistoric landscape.**

When the previous visitor centre was destroyed by a fire in May 2000, it took time to decide on a suitable design. The Giant's Causeway welcomes hundreds of thousands of visitors each year, so facilities must be able to cater for these numbers, whilst also giving adequate space for information about an attraction as large and complex as the Causeway. The site must of course be managed responsibly, as the Causeway is a designated UNESCO World Heritage Site (see previous page), so a sustainable, environmentally considerate design was required.

The unique design of the Giant's Causeway visitor centre was the result of an international architecture competition, won by Dublin-based firm heneghan peng. Large as it is, with great and detailed consideration to its many design features, it took just 18 months to construct and is built to last 100 years.

Above The unique design and precision engineering of the basalt façades create a unique pattern which echoes the shapes found in the Causeway's natural basalt columns

## Most ingenious engineering

Even without the knowledge of what lies beyond this gateway, the visitor is put in mind of the columns of the Causeway. The basalt façades are precisely engineered to create a unique pattern, which echoes the shapes found in the Causeway's natural basalt columns. There is not a single right angle in the building; the architects designed a series of non-repeating patterns, which meant the blocks had to be finished by hand and carefully slotted together like a giant jigsaw.

But as it echoes it also blends, appearing to rise out of the landscape and capped with grass to match the swards of the fields all around. And it is literally connected with the landscape, as the construction of the visitor centre restored the 'ridgeline', allowing visitors to walk an unbroken line from Runkerry, across the visitor centre roof and on to the Shepherd's Steps and beyond. The roof also serves to harvest rainwater, used to flush the toilets. As you might expect, the building is designed to be as sustainable as possible: nearly 5 km (3 miles) of pipe runs underneath the car park to provide ground-source heat; and 1 km (0.6 miles) of pipe, as wide as a metre in places, is also buried underground, drawing in air to cool the visitor centre.

## Explore some more

There is an enormous amount of information available in the visitor centre, which you can lightly browse or fully immerse yourself in. There's also, of course, somewhere to sit and take refreshment, buy a souvenir or two, or even take shelter from the occasionally wild weather of the North Antrim coast.

You may even be perusing this guidebook, whether to glean what's in store before stepping out onto the Causeway, or to learn more about the fascinating things you've seen.

So now we've learned about how the Causeway and its landscape came to be, let's find out more about the stories of the Causeway and the people who told them.

Right The visitor centre is an architectural statement that, while striking, is also sympathetic to its environment

# The Cause of Much Inspiration

While the geologists, scientists and volcanologists debate the origins of the Causeway, to some people there is only one version of events. The Causeway was clearly the work of a giant, and the remains of his titanic efforts continue to inspire those who come to walk in his footsteps.

# The story of Finn McCool

**When humans first laid eyes on the Causeway they assumed it could only be the work of giants, hence the name. The naming of the giant as Finn McCool (or *Finn mac Cumhaill* in Irish) seems to have started with the tales that were written down in the 1840s, but as with all the best stories, there are many versions told. Here is just one.**

Finn McCool was a giant who, for the most part, lived a quiet life with his family here on the Northern Irish coast. But there were rivals, other giants, and perhaps to pre-empt a challenge from his Scottish neighbour, Benandonner, Finn laid down the gauntlet and then built the Giant's Causeway so they could meet to do battle.

However, on his way over to Scotland, Finn spied Benandonner in the distance and realised that his rival was much bigger, taller and stronger than he had appeared from across the water. Finn decided he didn't want to fight Benandonner any more and ran back home as fast as he could – so fast that he lost his boot on the shore (see right).

Finn found his wife Oonagh and explained the terrible mistake he had made. Oonagh, being the brains of the pair, devised the plan of dressing Finn up as a baby and putting him into their son Oisín's cot, covering him with blankets and wrapping a shawl around his head.

Just then there was a loud banging at the door – Benandonner! 'Where's Finn?' he demanded, 'I want to fight him!'

'Calm down!' said Oonagh, 'Finn's out herding the cows. Why don't you come and wait for him and I'll make you a cup of tea?'

So Benandonner had his cup of tea but then grew impatient again. 'Where's Finn?' he roared. Oonagh explained again, 'He is out herding the cows but while you're here why don't you let me introduce you to our son Oisín?'

When Benandonner saw the giant baby in the cot he got scared. He thought, if that's the size of the baby, how big is the father?

Benandonner immediately ran out of the house and home across the Causeway, tearing it behind him to make sure Finn couldn't follow him. The other end of the Giant's Causeway still exists today on the Island of Staffa (see page 6).

Left The Causeway – a giant's walkway?

Above Certainly gigantic boots to fill

# The origin of Finn

**Finn McCool was a mythical hunter-warrior of Irish mythology, occurring also in the mythologies of Scotland and the Isle of Man. *Fionn* means 'blond' or 'fair'. Stories of this fair-haired warrior were told long before they were transcribed by monks around the 1100s, forming the Fenian Cycle (*an Fhiannaíocht*), much of it narrated in the voice of Finn's son, the poet Oisín.**

Most of Finn's early adventures are recounted in *The Boyhood Deeds of Finn*. He was the son of Cumhaill, leader of the Fianna tribe, and Muirne, the daughter of a druid. The young Finn studied under the druid and poet Finnéces, who had spent seven years trying to catch the Salmon of Knowledge. Eventually Finnéces caught the salmon, and told his pupil to cook it for him.

While cooking the fish, Finn burned his thumb, instinctively putting it in his mouth, thereby gaining all the knowledge in the world and investing him with the qualities to become one of Irish folklore's favourite heroes.

## Growing in stature

More popular tales were told about Finn than any other hero – one tells of him scooping up part of Ireland to fling it at a rival, but missing so it landed in the Irish Sea, forming the Isle of Man – so when the first storytellers were looking to identify the creator of the Giant's Causeway, Finn was the obvious choice, and he consequently grew in stature from hunter-warrior to giant.

Above From T. W. Rolleston's *The High Deeds of Finn and other Bardic Romances of Ancient Ireland*, illustrated by Stephen Reid, 1910

Left Finn with the Salmon of Knowledge; illustration by H. R. Millar from *Celtic Myth and Legend by Charles Squire*, 1905

'What Irish man, woman, or child has not heard of our renowned Hibernian Hercules, the great and glorious Fin M'Coul?'

William Carleton, 1845

# A long-lost love story

As we said, versions of the story of Finn McCool and the Giant's Causeway abound. Each new generation adds their own embellishments to the story. This is exactly what the Causeway guides did in their day, as we'll see later. But for those who prefer a love story to one of quarrelling giants, here's an entirely different version.

The tale previously told was only written down for the first time in the 1840s, by an anonymous contributor to a newspaper called *The Dublin Penny Journal*. The alternative story told by Causeway guides in the 1700s and early 1800s – of Finn building the Causeway for love rather than pride – was thought lost. Then a poem came to light – in a library in Trondheim, Norway, of all places – written by Mary Anne Allingham of Ballyshannon after a visit to the Causeway in 1830. The tale she was told by her guides is as follows:

'Finn had fallen in love with a Scottish maiden. Sad that he couldn't reach her, he walked along the shore, skimming stones across the sea. Seeing them spin out to sea, Finn hit upon a plan – he would build a Causeway to reach his love. Finn worked all day, and made good progress, extending the Causeway nearly halfway across the sea. Tired, he went home to bed, confident he would finish the job the next day.

However, his grandmother had other ideas. Afraid of losing him, she used her magic to call up an enormous storm to destroy what Finn had built. Finn woke the next day to find his Causeway in ruins. Undaunted, he started anew. Once more the stones stretched out into the ocean, but that very night his work was destroyed. Finn tried again and again: the harder he laboured, the more violent the storms.

Close to exhaustion, he made one last attempt, building on through the night. The storms rose up around Finn, tearing at him with thunder and lightening, while wild waves beat at every rock he tried to lift. At last he reached the other side; but the trial was too much, even for a giant. He fell down and died in the arms of his beloved. Behind him the Causeway slipped below the waves for a final time. Finn's Granny climbed to the top of a headland to see what had happened. Horrified by what her magic had done, she turned to stone. She stands there to this day.'

# The Causeway's reputation grows

**Susanna Drury's paintings of the Giant's Causeway in 1739–40 captured the imagination of a public fascinated and delighted by her accurate yet romantic depictions of this natural wonder. More artists would follow, as well as writers, poets and novelists to help spread the word.**

## Mary Delany

Mary Delany (1700–88) was an English artist, courtier and lady of letters, corresponding with the great figures of her day including not only King George III and Queen Charlotte, but also the author Jonathan Swift, the composer George Frideric Handel and philosopher Jean-Jacques Rousseau. Mary recorded her travels in a huge volume of letters, diaries and sketches. She visited the Causeway in 1758, after many months of planning. Her first sight of the Causeway left her uncharacteristically short of words – 'I am now quite at a loss to give you an idea of it; it is so different from anything I ever saw' – but she later found them and left us a full account along with sketches of what she saw.

'We are just returned from seeing the most wonderful sight that, perhaps, is to be seen in the world.'

Mary Delany

Right **Mary Delany** was an early and well-connected visitor to the Causeway

## W. M. Thackeray

William Makepeace Thackeray (1811–63) was a great English author, most famous for the novel *Vanity Fair* (1847). He visited the Causeway in 1842 and his account of it in his *Irish Sketchbook* is full of the acerbic humour and biting sarcasm that can be seen in his famous satire of 19th-century society. Here is what he had to say about his first foray to the Causeway: 'The traveller no sooner issues from the inn [the Causeway Hotel] by a back door, which he is informed will lead him straight to the Causeway, than the guides pounce upon him, with a dozen rough boatmen, who are likewise lying in wait; and a crew of shrill beggar-boys with boxes of spars [specimens] ready to tear him and each other to pieces seemingly, yell and bawl incessantly round him.'

He also had a rough time of it on his boat tour – more of that later – but it's likely that his account of the Causeway drew more visitors to see this wild, rough-hewn wonder for themselves.

'The hill tops are shattered into a thousand cragged fantastical shapes; the water comes swelling into scores of little strange creeks, or goes off with a leap, roaring into those mysterious caves yonder.'

W. M. Thackeray

## The Earl Bishop

Simultaneously the Earl of Bristol and Bishop of Derry, Frederick Hervey (1730–1803) was an extremely influential and wealthy man, who did much to put the Causeway 'on the map'. He would insist on bringing all his guests – he had his estate at Downhill Demesne in County Derry~Londonderry – to the Causeway, and he paid for the first access road to the columns. Previously the only access to the shore was by rough single tracks. The Earl's carriageway fell into disrepair after his death, but it remains the basis of the road used by millions of visitors today.

Above **Frederick Hervey, 4th Earl of Bristol and Bishop of Derry, did much to promote the Causeway as a visitor attraction**

Right **The novelist William Makepeace Thackeray published a mixed account of his visit to the Causeway**

# Garrulous guides

**Once word was out, visitors flocked to see this exciting, newly discovered landscape. There they found a ready supply of guides, all with their own stories, happy to entertain, bemuse and bewilder these wide-eyed and hopefully deep-pocketed visitors.**

As long ago as 1708 an account of a visit to the Causeway by Samuel Molyneux (nephew of the famous Thomas, see page 8) says that the party 'tooke a Guide'. So just a decade after its 'discovery' by Samuel's uncle, enterprising locals had seen an opportunity to supplement their incomes. They'd start guiding as young as 15 or 16 and some would still be reeling off their tales into their 80s, perhaps without even repeating the same one twice! Generations of guides would follow, inheriting their fathers' tips and tricks and tales, but also adding their own twists for the tourists' entertainment.

'Alexander Anderson from Dundee found David McConaghy extremely civil and attentive and one of the most intelligent guides I ever met.'
15 August 1870

'We have seen the two caverns at the causeway under the guidance of John McConaghy, who has served us well in a most severe rainstorm.'
Isaac G. Kendall and family, U.S.A.
5 September 1870

'I guarantee David McConaghy free from the usual humbug & blarney which is generally found in his profession. In fact a guide in the true sense of the term.'
W. Watson, 15 July 1873

'The guide performed his office satisfactorily and most obligingly but it would be an improvement if guides could be bought to describe natural appearance correctly and to omit the senseless jargon about Giants.' President of the Geological Society of Glasgow, 7 April 1876

Right The Stookans and the honeycomb of the Middle Causeway

Opposite Guides at rest (left to right): Johnny Martin, Robert Colvin, James McMullan, and Willie Colvin with Johnny McLernon at the back of the Royal Hotel in 1952

## The classic tour

When the Causeway tram became fully operational in 1887 (see page 12–13), even with visitor numbers higher than they'd ever been, competition between the guides was fierce, with rich pickings from visitors wealthy enough to travel for recreation. In an account of 1884, the fee was half a crown (about 12p), or 'as much more as your honour pleases'.

For this fee the classic itinerary of the 1890s offered, as described by guide Alexander McMullan: 'If the sea was calm and they were willing to go, I would take [the visitors] to the boats … [otherwise] I took them down … the 'Quality Rodden' [the road to the Causeway] … we went past 'the Stookans' … [and] turned down to the well – some [visitors] partook of refreshment and some did not … after that I took them on to the 'wishing chair' and … the top of the 'Honeycomb' and pointed out the 'Giant's Organ' in the distance…. I then took [visitors onto] the Grand Causeway and showed … the most perfect pentagon on the Causeway, and then to the 'Lady's fan' which is said to belong to the giant's wife. We went then to the 'Keystone'…. [My Customers] would sometimes go by the Shepherd's Path, and sometimes would take a stroll by a longer path, round to Pleaskin's Head … but very few would try that.'

Already by this time dozens of features had been designated, each with a tall tale attached, but they were unlikely to be consistent between guides, each preferring his own if he thought it more entertaining; and really, nothing very much has changed!

## A new era

The glory days of the guides were from the 1860s to the 1940s. After the Second World War everything had changed and visitor numbers declined. By 1949 the tram to the Causeway had closed due to lack of business, and many guides returned to fishing, labouring and farming.

But the connection was not entirely lost. When the care of the Giant's Causeway became the National Trust's, one guide in particular, the 'King of the Causeway' no less, stayed to carry on the tradition. Alec Martin was well known on the Causeway – 'sometime guide, carver of wishing chair souvenirs, plausible ne'er-do-well and distiller of poteen' – who was telling his stories well into the 1970s.

The National Trust staff and volunteers, who now look after the Causeway and its visitors, all live locally and many were born nearby. All know the history of the 'Causey' guides and keep the old stories alive, while possibly throwing in a few new ones of their own!

# Sightseeing from the sea

GIANT'S EYE GLASS. CAUSEWAY. 5887. W.L

**Many guides also acted as boatmen, and for over 100 years a boat tour was an essential part of any visit. These vessels were expertly piloted by the boatmen in frequently choppy, if not downright dangerous waters, who somehow maintained the patter while keeping their fares afloat.**

There were about 10 boats in service and the trip started at the Brenther in Portnaboe (see page 34) and then headed west to the caves of Runkerry, before going east to see the Causeway from the sea. Passengers were sometimes landed onto the Grand Causeway itself. In 1842 famous author W. M. Thackeray paid 10 shillings (see box opposite), but prices appeared to have varied widely and according to what the punter was prepared to pay.

## More to explore

The seven-metre (20-feet) rowboats could take up to 20 passengers, with up to four oarsmen if conditions were particularly tricky. Once embarked at the Brenther, holding onto wooden posts obligingly set into holes in the slippery rock, tourists would be first taken to Portcoon cave. There the passengers could marvel at the caves before having the wits scared out of them by a single gunshot, fired to demonstrate the cave's acoustics. While they were still dazed, a long-handled butterfly net would be waved in front of them by the gunman in the cave, and they might drop in a few coins. Next was Runkerry cave – reputedly the largest sea-cave in Ireland – and the boat would venture in as deeply as the swell or the boatman's nerve would allow.

Above The Giant's Eyeglass in the 1890s

From there the passengers would be propelled back to Portnaboe, around the looming Stookans and on to Port Ganny, where they would finally set eyes on the Causeway. The short tour would disembark there, to be met by various vendors, hawkers and well keepers (see over). However, the longer version would carry on to the Amphitheatre, on past Port na Spaniagh and the Giant's Eyeglass. This last feature is lost now, but it was an oval-shaped sea arch, which collapsed in 1948.

The Long Course reached its farthest extent with a chance to view the soaring headland of Pleaskin (meaning high, unsheltered land), four bays (around two miles) beyond the Causeway columns. This headland is much higher and steeper than the headland behind the Grand Causeway (see Aird Snout on page 38). With perfect tiers of basalt columns and other strata, it looks like the layers of a giant wedding cake. Many visitors of the 1800s were much more moved by Pleaskin Head than by the Causeway columns.

## Boat tours no more

As with the land-based guides' tours, boat tours declined dramatically after the Second World War. By the time the National Trust took over the care of the Causeway in 1961, there had been no boat tours in five or six years, and many of the boatmen were gone. The Trust explored reviving the tradition of boat tours in the late 1960s, partially renovating the Brenther, but it was ultimately decided that the impact and costs of building a modern slipway were just too great.

### An intrepid tourist

Author W. M. Thackeray visited the Causeway in 1842. An intrepid and curious sort of tourist, he braved the boat trip and left us this account: 'For after all, it must be remembered it is pleasure we come for – that we are not obliged to take these boats. Well, well! I paid ten shillings for mine, and ten minutes before would cheerfully have paid five pounds to be allowed to quit it.' He even sketched the episode, which was later engraved and included in his *Irish Sketchbook*. Thackeray has drawn himself, quite composed in his top hat, sitting on the left in the prow of the storm-tossed boat.

# A booming trade

**The guides and boatmen made a decent living at the Causeway, but there was also a variety of other characters who would offer a service and generally an accompanying story in exchange for a shilling or two.**

There is a tiny freshwater pool near the Little Causeway called the Giant's Well, bordered by hexagonal stones (see also page 36). Rather than a spring it's more likely rainwater that has run off the slopes of the headland above. But that didn't stop it quickly becoming a key feature of the Causeway visit, naturally attributed to Finn the Giant who used it to quench his thirst.

## All the Old Marys

Its reputation and magical properties were promoted by a series of well keepers, invariably women, generally elderly, more than one of whom had the same name, so all well keepers came to be known as Old Marys. She would charge visitors for a glass of water and a wish. Some Old Marys would offer a chaser with the water, some local whiskey to please the tourists.

This practice died out in the 1950s due to health concerns, as the water was found to be contaminated, probably by something unsavoury washed off the fields.

'The water is in every respect really delicious. The well is always presided over by some old person – a native of the place – who makes a fair livelihood for supplying tourists with draughts of water.'

Harry MacAlister Jr, 1887

### An Irish archetype

Long before the well business dried up there was a bevy of souvenir sellers, also generally local women, who would set up their stalls on the columns of the Causeway. Many, responding to visitors' scientific curiosity about the place, would offer 'specimens'. These were stones gathered from the Causeway but the genuineness of their provenance could not always be relied upon. Some souvenir sellers even bought in fossils (which aren't found in Causeway rocks) from the Jurassic Coast in Devon and Dorset to keep up with increasing demand and to catch the eye of their customers in a competitive market.

The specimens were immortalised in a popular song, 'Little Irish Nell', and so Nell became an archetype for the souvenir sellers:

'Do buy a box of specimens, and take
    me for your guide,
I'll point you out all that's to be seen
    along the Causeway side;
I'll lead you to the Magic Well, and to
    the Giant's Chair,
And ALL will surely come to pass you
    wish when seated there.
Who'll give a shilling for a box? I really
    wish to sell.
Do buy a box of specimens from
    Little Irish Nell.'

Opposite **An Old Mary by the Giant's Well**

Left **Little Irish Nell depicted on a postcard**

Right **The Chalet girls in the 1950s**

### 'Fatal to small silver'

That's how one visitor described a visit to the Causeway in a guide's logbook. It's true there was no shortage of opportunities for visitors to spend their money. By the mid-1800s the souvenir sellers had expanded their wares to include postcards and booklets, linen and lace. These were sold from small shops, known as 'tents' (even though they were made from wood and corrugated iron), which proliferated over the next 60 years, as did the variety of souvenirs on offer. A larger and more permanent 'tent', the Chalet was a tearoom situated in Port Noffer, which served visitors for over 50 years.

Today's visitors have to wait until they get back to the visitor centre to buy their souvenirs and refreshments, but there they'll find distinctive, quality products – locally sourced whenever possible – sold by locals, hopefully maintaining some of the spirit of the souvenir sellers.

# The art of the Causeway

From Susanna Drury's first depictions of the Causeway, this extraordinary landscape has fired the imaginations of many who set eyes upon it and wondered about its creation. Here are just a few of the more memorable images it has inspired.

**1.** John Nixon (c.1750–1818) is thought to have been born in Belfast, but moved to London in 1784 and exhibited frequently at the Royal Academy. He visited Ireland on several occasions during the 1780s and 1790s, and produced a series of drawings and watercolours all over the north of Ireland.

**2.** A few decades later, another Belfast man, Andrew Nicholl (1804–86), was drawn to the Causeway and produced dozens of paintings and engravings from 1828 onwards. The second son of a boot and shoemaker, he taught and practised landscape drawing in London, Dublin and Belfast.

**3.** The Causeway came in reach of the railways as early as 1855. Railway companies commissioned beautiful illustrated posters to advertise their services to Ireland and the Causeway. Perhaps the most iconic posters were created during the 1930s, but they continued to be made well into the 1960s. This one by John Greene was published in 1960.

**4.** A local artist with an international reputation, James McKendry has painted the Causeway many times. This handfinished print was created exclusively for the Causeway in 2012 so it could be included in the newly built visitor centre.

**5.** Jamie Hageman is a British mountain landscape painter, based in the West Highlands of Scotland. Self-taught, his work earned him a place among the finalists of Sky Arts' Landscape Artist of the Year 2015. The incredible detail in his painting shows the degree of his fascination with these raw and exposed places.

# The Causeway Today

So we've seen what the scientists have to say about the Causeway and the tales and art that this remarkable coastline has inspired, now it's time to see for ourselves. Let's take a tour to the Giant's Bay, with some stops along the way.

The Giant's Marbles before the Middle Causeway; the Giant's Chimneys are just discernible in the distance

# Portnaboe

**The first bay you come to from the visitor centre is Portnaboe, or the Bay of the Cow. But curiously it's not a cow that has captured people's imagination here but a four-legged creature of a kind uncommon in this part of Northern Ireland.**

Portnaboe got its name from the days when farmers grazed their cattle on the grassy lower slopes. But it is not only farmers who made good use of the landscape of the Causeway. In the bay are the remains of a series of low walls running parallel to the shore. These were 'kelp walls', where collected seaweed was hung to dry. It was then burned in nearby kilns and sold for a variety of uses including as a water softener, in glass making and for bleaching, including the production of world-famous Irish linen.

## Other enterprising uses

In Portnaboe is a narrow inlet called the Brenther. There is such a collection of names for all the curiosities of the Causeway and you might fairly assume they all come from Gaelic, but in fact 'brenther' comes from a Norse word meaning 'steep harbour'. Sadly there is no direct proof of Viking visits to the Causeway, although archaeologists have found Viking objects elsewhere on this coast.

What does remain at the Brenther is evidence of seafarers many centuries later. You'll recall in the last chapter that local boatmen saw tourist numbers increasing and subsequently saw an opportunity to make money (see page 26)? At the Brenther are pieces of an old winch that was used to pull the boats that took tourists on tours of the Causeway. You can also see the post-holes that were cut to help visitors across the slippery rocks.

## A curious creature

And what of that curious four-legged creature that has made this bay his home? If you look back towards Runkerry Head as you move on from Portnaboe, you'll see **the Camel**. One story goes that Finn found himself far from the Causeway one day and needed to get home in a hurry. So of course he hailed a giant galloping camel. Other explanations claim that the Camel is actually a dyke of hard basalt, formed from cooling lava that pushed its way up through layers of softer rock that wore away over hundreds of thousands of years, leaving the Camel.

Below The Bay of the Cow is home to the Camel, a dyke of dolerite

# Port Ganny

**Port Ganny owes its name to the fact that it's the only bay of the Causeway with any sand – the Irish word for sand is *gaineamh*. It's not a lot of sand and there's perhaps less than there was, as farmers used to take sand from here to use on their heavy clay soils.**

What Sandy Bay lacks in sand it makes up for in fascinating features, each with its own enigmatic name and fanciful tale. **The Windy Gap**, which the road runs through as it passes between Portnaboe and Port Ganny, is said to be the windiest place in Ireland. Quite a claim! Also between Portnaboe and Port Ganny is the top of the headland known as **Weir's Snout**. This can be accessed using the red trail and affords stunning views.

## Tall tales

There are two features in Port Ganny related to Finn, one being his very own grandmother! If you look back from the eastern part of Port Ganny and the light is right, you can see **Granny**, her back stooped as she makes her slow way up the slope (see page 21).

Further along this same headland you'll see **the Stookans**, twin hills. 'Stookan' or 'Steucan' (it can also be spelt 'Steuchan') is the Ulster-Scots word for haystack. So apparently Finn was a farmer as well as a builder, but his decision to put his haystacks so close to the sea suggests he was better at constructing causeways!

### Onion skins

These features can be spotted in various locations along the Causeway, but the best examples are probably here in Port Ganny. Stop at the Windy Gap and look back towards the visitor centre and you'll see them on your left at the bottom of Weir's Snout. These rocks have been exposed as the softer rock around them has been worn away. The surface of each stone has then undergone a long process of chemical weathering, which creates thin outer layers of degraded rock, which 'peel' off like the layers of an onion, hence the name. If you miss them, you can find a picture of them on the back cover.

Above Port Ganny; if you look very closely you can see Granny making her way up the slope on the right

# The Little Causeway

**The Giant's Causeway is actually divided into three parts – the Little, Middle and Grand Causeways – separated from one another by dykes made of harder rock, which formed after the columns themselves. The Little Causeway, with its shallow rock pools and flattish surface, might be overlooked and can only be reached with care.**

Little this causeway may be, but there are still remains of the giant scattered about. Apparently when not at work building his causeway or haystacks, Finn enjoyed a game of marbles. **The Giant's Marbles** litter the ground near the Little Causeway, huge stones rounded by years of erosion and weathering. In geological rather than mythological terms, their make-up suggests that they may well be pieces of a broken-up basalt dyke.

## A once well-known place

**The Giant's Well** is a tiny freshwater pool bordered by hexagon-shaped basalt stones. Its reputation and place in local history are larger than the well itself, as it was once an essential part of a visit to the Causeway, largely owing to the presence of the well keeper (see page 28). At one time the keepers even gave a 'free' shot of whiskey with the glasses of water they sold.

Its popularity meant the area around the well was altered, with column stones moved to form a set of seats. The water was proved to be unsafe to drink in the 1950s, and the well was largely filled in with the re-surfacing of the road to the Causeway in the 1970s.

The well is not featured on tours due to the danger of rock falls in this area. Instead, refreshment awaits in the visitor centre, or The Nook if something stronger is preferred!

Above The Giant's Marbles in front of the Little Causeway

Opposite The Wishing Chair

# The Middle Causeway

**This causeway is perhaps the most-photographed part of the Giant's Causeway on account of its remarkable honeycomb appearance. Millions of visitors have followed in the giant's footsteps as they take the exhilarating, and often slippery, walk as far as they dare.**

If the Giant's Well was once a compulsory part of the tour, **the Wishing Chair** is now an essential stop and photo opportunity. The Wishing Chair is a natural throne, its tall back formed by the smooth sides of three columns, while two well-positioned 'arm rests' make this a seat fit for a king. Indeed, it has been the seat, briefly, of royalty, when Prince Charles visited in 1996. Northern Ireland's First and Deputy First Ministers Peter Robinson and Martin McGuiness sat in the chair at the opening of the new visitor centre in 2012. Prime Minister David Cameron visited during the Olympics in 2012, his wish perhaps boosting the success of Team GB that year.

### Wishing rules

At one time the rule was that only women could sit in the Wishing Chair, but there are still three rules the wisher must adhere to, as one local man, Elliott Houston, explains: 'The first one is that you have to keep it a secret, otherwise it won't work. The second rule is you mustn't wish for too much: 'I wish I could win the lottery' – it won't happen! The third rule … is that as you make your wish, you have to wiggle your bottom three times! Now that's why the stone's so shiny, you see. Everybody thinks that's rubbish but it's not rubbish. You ask the Argentinean youth football team that came to play here in the Milk Cup a number of years ago. Every one of them got into that wishing chair and they all made their wish, just according to the rules and they WON the tournament! Not only then, but two years in a row! Need I say more?' Pictured above is a group of tourists in the 1950s when the Wishing Chair was marked out with chalk.

# The Grand
Causeway

**Finally, the Grand Causeway. This is the largest collection of columns, the remains of Finn's mighty 'pavement' curving gently out to sea and Scotland. Here you'll find many other gigantic features – the old guides appear to have saved all their best stories for this part of the tour!**

One rather sweet feature found on top of the Grand Causeway is **the Giant's Fan**. A set of sunken stones, perfectly pentagonal in shape, form a delicate fan shape, which sometimes fills with water after stormy weather. This is said to be the imprint of a fan, which Finn gave his wife Oonagh.

But as we know, Finn was a fighter as well as a lover, and he had **the Giant's Cannons** at the ready, horizontal columns aimed across the sea in case Benandonner came back. Less obvious than they once were owing to rock falls and the subsequent growth of vegetation, you'll find them poking out from the lower middle part of Aird Snout, the imposing headland found directly behind the columns of the Grand Causeway.

Left Aird Snout looming high behind the Grand Causeway

Above A postcard of the Giant's Fan, c.1905

Right The Giant's Loom

## Towering above

**The Giant's Gate** is the name for the gap between the Grand Causeway and the slopes of the Aird headland above, which allows access through to the next bay, Port Noffer. Some say it was cut by Finn after he had built the Causeway, to keep him from stubbing his toe as he made his way from bay to bay. However, a more prosaic explanation says the gate was cut in 1852 by Mr Hugh Lecky, who owned a long lease on the Causeway. Finding a section of the Grand Causeway rather inconvenient for access to Port Noffer, he removed a slice of it!

However, any disappointment arising from that story is soon put aside when you see what is just around the corner. **The Giant's Loom**, located on the Port Noffer side of the Grand Causeway, is a long array of towering columns about half a metre (two feet) in diameter, the tallest of which is 10 metres (33 feet) in height. The old guides used to claim it was used by Finn 'for weaving his garters on'.

# Port Noffer

**Port Noffer means 'the Giant's Bay', so called as the tradition is that this is where Finn the giant had his family home. Folklore it may be, but the McCool family left the evidence of their domestic life littered around for all to see, and the chimneys of their house are in plain view.**

Perhaps the bay's most famous feature and one that has had a variety of tales told about it is **the Giant's Boot**. This was discarded by Finn in his flight from the Scottish giant Benandonner (see page 19). It can only be a giant's boot as it has been estimated to equal a size 93½! Given the size of the loom he used to weave his garters, this is hardly surprising. Some years ago, Phillip Watson, former National Trust Warden at the Causeway, sought out a professional to calculate Finn's height. After discussions with numerous scientific institutes in Ireland, Britain and the US, expert opinion has it that, judging from his boot, Finn was over 16 metres, or 54 feet tall.

'The giant who made that organ for his diversion had a grand idea of music.'
Reverend Canon Hugh Forde, 1928

Above The Giant's Organ with columns up to 12 metres (40 feet) tall

Left The Giant's Chimneys

Right Oisín's Teddy Bear

Far right The Shepherd's Steps reward effort with a magnificent view

Whatever you choose to believe, it's undoubtedly an unmissable photo opportunity: the Victorians knew it as the 'Giant's Chair' for the reason that it makes a fine and comfortable seat from which to take in the surroundings.

## Finn's family life

**The Giant's Chimneys** of the McCool family home can be seen from various places in Port Ganny and Port Noffer, looking up at the headlands to the east. Judging by historic paintings and photos, sections of the chimneys have fallen down in the last hundred years. The loss of some of the Giant's Chimneys is part of the on-going process of erosion which left them protruding in the first place.

On the lower part of the headland below the Giant's Chimneys, harder to spot but obvious once you see its distinctive ears, is **the Teddy Bear** that belonged to Finn's son Oisín. Perhaps Oisín would play while his father sat at **the Giant's Organ** of an evening. In the side of the cliff opposite the Grand Causeway, it takes its name from the clear resemblance to a pipe organ, the columns that make the pipes at around 12 metres (40 feet) tall.

## A dangerous occupation

From Port Noffer you can retrace your steps and take the bus back to the visitor centre. Alternatively, you can take **the Shepherd's Steps**, all 162 of them. As the name suggests, this was a path once trodden by local shepherds. Barely wide enough for a man to walk with a sheep on his shoulders, as many would, the path claimed several lives. When the National Trust took over care of the Causeway in the 1960s, a band of plucky locals were employed to build the steps and make the path safe. They even wrote a poem about it:

> 'The Shepherd's path will be re-made,
> With rails and steps so grand
> Where tourists will, from this great view,
> See Innishtrahull's[1] fair land.'

1 The most northerly of Ireland's islands

# Port na Spaniagh

**Our tour along the coast of the Giant's Causeway ends in a bay with an enigmatic history. Its name, the start of which is marked by Roveran Valley Head, now seems an obvious clue as to what it is now famous for, yet one that oddly escaped treasure hunters for hundreds of years.**

On Roveran Valley Head is a seat that commemorates the sinking of the *Girona*, a ship that was part of the disastrous Spanish Armada of 1588. To give it its full title, the *Grande y Felicisima Armada* (translated as the 'Great and Most Fortunate Navy') was not the success its commander, the Duke of Medina Sidonia, hoped it would be. A total of 130 ships sailed to England with the aim of overthrowing Queen Elizabeth I and Protestantism. However, a fleet of English fireships scattered the Spanish off the coast of Northern France and forced them to flee northwards, up and around Scotland, away from hostile English waters but into the storms of the North Atlantic, where many ships were sunk.

## Few were spared

The *Girona* was among these and met her end during a storm on the night of 26 October. Her rudder smashed, she hit the low-lying rocks of Lacada Point and was torn apart. Another misunderstood name, Lacada was once mistaken for Spanish but it is in fact derived from the Gaelic *Leac Fhada*, meaning 'long flagstone'.

Of the 1,300 sailors on board the *Girona*, just five survived. Their rescuer was James McDonnell of nearby Dunluce Castle (no friend of the English crown), who conveyed the survivors to Scotland over the following months. However, there are stories of some of the survivors staying at Dunluce for a year or more and at least one Portballintrae family claims descent from the *Girona* crew. There are also stories that McDonnell used the proceeds of salvage from the ship to make improvements to his castle.

Above Lacada Point where the *Girona* fatefully foundered

Left English ships and the Spanish Armada, August 1588. The *Girona* was a galleass, higher, larger and slower than regular galleys, similar to that pictured in the middle foreground

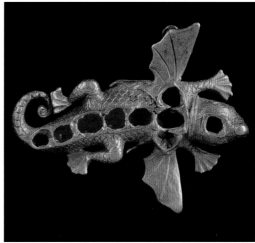

Top right Found at the wreck site, a salamander of gold set with rubies. These creatures were believed to be impervious to fire, so were carried for good luck by sailors of wooden ships

## Uncovering secrets

So the residents of Portballintrae certainly knew the full story, but preferred to keep the details and the location of the wreck and her treasures to themselves. Over the following centuries, many came in search of the *Girona*, but none was successful. It wasn't until 1968 that a Belgian marine archaeologist asked the right questions of the right people – the locals – and struck gold, literally and metaphorically.

Robert Stenuit was staying at Portballintrae while investigating the area. The story goes that his photographer, Marc Jasinski, thought to pick up a one and threepenny guidebook. In it was written: 'In 1588 … the galleass *Girona* was wrecked at a little cove near the Giant's Causeway, still called Port na Spaniagh.' Marc showed this fresh evidence to Robert who, once he had picked himself up off the floor, planned the next dive.

By the time Robert and his team found the site of the wreck, there was virtually nothing left of the wooden ship, and artefacts had been scattered over a large area. They spent over 6,000 hours recovering 12,000 items. The first thing they found was a lead ingot, the raw material for cannon and musket balls, but better was to follow and they recovered fabulous rings, gold and silver chains and elaborate protective amulets carried by the sailors to keep them safe at sea. These precious items can be seen in all their glory at the Ulster Museum, as part of an exhibition that tells the story of the *Girona* and her crew.

### A survivor's search

Another survivor of a different wreck of the Armada was Francisco de Cuellar. He was also shipwrecked in Ireland and later wrote an account of his search for fellow survivors. He evidently learned of the fate of the *Girona*, writing: 'I went to the huts of some savages that were there, who told me of the great misfortunes of our people who were drowned at that place, and showed me many jewels and valuables of theirs, which distressed me greatly.'

# In the seas

**So far we've focused on what we can see above sea level, but the waters of the Giant's Causeway Coast are every bit as important. Indeed, without their erosive effect the coastline of the Causeway would look very different. But you don't even have to get your feet wet to find out more about what lies beneath the waves.**

Some of the watery residents of the coast are easier to spot; others, while suitably gigantic, are harder to see. At the sea's edge live brittle starfish and crabs. Plaice and dab swim close to shore. A little further out, wrasse can be found. Further still are larger creatures, like seals and porpoises, who pay the occasional visit. However, from around May, the biggest sea dweller off the coast of the Causeway is easily the basking shark. Reaching up to 12 metres (40 feet) in length, with mouths up to a metre (three feet) wide and the larger of their two distinctive dorsal fins as big, they could be a terrifying sight but they feed only on microscopic plankton.

## Underwater forests

We've seen the many enterprises that the Causeway has supported over hundreds of years, and one particularly abundant resource in these parts are the huge kelp forests. The conditions off this coast mean a variety of kelp thrives here, some of them growing tens of metres tall. The cooler waters of the Atlantic meet nutrient-rich waters coming north from the Irish Sea and create the best kelp habitat in Europe. Anchored to rocks by structures called holdfasts, kelps are tough enough to survive storms, waves, drying out and changes in temperature. These enormous forests provide food and shelter for numerous animals, such as crabs, urchins, limpets, sponges, brittle stars and blennies, many of which use the forest as a safe place in which to raise their young. At low tide you may even find, entwined in the kelp, mermaid's purses, the egg cases of skates, sharks and rays.

Left The metre-wide mouth of a basking shark drawing in plankton

Right (top to bottom) Blue-rayed limpets appear deceptively tropical

The common brittle star varies in colour, ranging from violet, purple or red to yellowish or pale grey, often spotted with red

The tompot blenny is less common but an example of the area's sometimes spectacular marine life

Below A young grey seal playing in the kelp

## Maritime mammals

It's not only fish that swim and breed off the coast, but also the mammals that feed on them. Two types of seals are often spotted in the waters around Northern Ireland: grey seals and common seals. You can best tell them apart by their noses: grey seals have long noses with straight nostrils, whereas common seals have V-shaped nostrils. Common seals, also known as harbour seals, are actually less so than grey seals.

The more commonly seen grey seals breed on the rocky coast around the Causeway from September to December, and can be spotted playing offshore. Seals are wary of humans, so they're seldom seen pulling up out of the water on the stacks and islands nearest to the Causeway, which is normally busy with visitors.

### Making a living by the seaside

People have settled on the north coast of Ireland for over 9,000 years, drawn to the area's plentiful resources, not least those under the sea. Salmon has been the catch of the day for generations, famously netted with the use of the rope bridge at Carrick-a-Rede, but also caught by fishermen based at Dunseverick and Aird Snout. Salmon used to be netted off Runkerry Head (you can still see the net house on the rocks at the Portballintrae side). It's certainly an industry with a history – Susanna Drury's paintings of the 1740s show game fishers using the Causeway as a platform and there are several other paintings of salmon fishers off the Causeway.

# In the skies

**The Causeway may appear a rocky, windswept place to take up residence, but its shoreline, craggy cliffs and cliff-top heaths and fields are full of food for the birds, making it a very attractive proposition and perch for many different species.**

**Eider ducks** make their nests in crevices on and around Causeway islets. The females paddle in around the Causeway bays with their young in late June and early July, while the males stay offshore looking for food and are best seen from October to May.

Another familiar sight around the coast are **oystercatchers**, many of whom live along the coast year round but whose numbers swell in the winter months. Easy to spot with their distinctive long red bill and legs, they make their nests in the open, some of them even on the columns of the Grand Causeway itself.

**Fulmars** now dominate the rocky cliffs of Runkerry Head, having colonised the site in the 1930s. They make their homes on narrow ledges and cracks, and have an unusual way of protecting their nests – they spit foul-smelling oil at anything that gets too close, so you've been warned!

## Farms and fields

**Wheatears** and **grasshopper warblers** both travel all the way from Africa to nest at the Causeway. The latter are endangered and rare this far north. They like damp grassland where they feed on insects, with spiders and woodlice being particular favourites.

**Stonechats** live in the heaths and fields of the Causeway cliff tops, where gorse provides them with shelter and insects for food. They get their name from their alarm call, which sounds like two stones being hit together.

**Reed buntings** are small farmland birds whose name comes from the males' habit of perching on the end of a long piece of stiff grass or reed to sing through the evening. Their numbers have declined elsewhere due to intensive farming practices, but the joint efforts of the National Trust and tenant farmers, who think and work sustainably, have ensured these birds have a home in the Causeway fields.

If reed bunting numbers are struggling, spare a thought for the **skylark**, which is on the threatened 'red' list. To lose them and their beautiful song would be a terrible thing, so again farming practices that are considerate of their habitat are followed at the Causeway.

Above clockwise
Eider duck, oystercatcher, fulmar, stonechat, grasshopper warbler, wheatear, reed bunting

# Beneath our feet

**The ability of species to adapt to the least likely of environments is remarkable. Even the rocks and thin soil close to the water's edge support a surprising amount of very determined vegetation.**

Lichens in particular love the rocky, salty surfaces of the Causeway. Slow-growing black, grey and yellow lichens coat many of the columns and nearby boulders. Lichens are actually made up of several organisms – a fungus and an algae working together in a symbiotic relationship. Oysterplant has managed to establish in the thin soils among the boulders and on the beaches of the Causeway. It has silvery-green leaves and produces tiny blue flowers in summer, and is rare elsewhere in the UK and Ireland.

Other plants take root in cracks between rocks, and in summer, clumps of sea pinks, sea campion and bird's-foot trefoil bring splashes of pink, white and yellow. Indeed, the effect of the bird's-foot trefoil has so charmed locals that they've given it a nickname – 'bacon and eggs'!

## Not so *terra firma*

These are just a few of the plants that have colonised the Causeway, but it is not a static environment and they must continue to adapt. Given the lashing the coast receives from the sea and sky, the occasional landslip is to be expected and has to be carefully managed to keep the Causeway safe for visitors and preserve the many habitats of countless species.

Plants in particular have to adapt to colonise this unstable environment. There are radically different timescales involved. A landslip can happen in minutes, yet while sections of soil scar (bare soil) may take a year or two to green over, it can take rocky scree slopes (boulders and stones) thousands of years to be fully covered with soil. However, given the Causeway's 60-million year history, this really is the blink of an eye.

Above Sea pinks on the North Antrim coastal path to the Causeway

Left Sections of scree following a landslip

# Nature has the last word

**So we've seen how the Causeway was formed, the millions who've come here and been moved to sing and write and take photos, and learned about the variety of wildlife that has made the Causeway home. But the story doesn't end here.**

The history of the Causeway may be millennia old, but its story is still being written. The story of its evolution, the movements of the Earth and the effects of its natural elements, the story of the people who have come and continue to come and be awestruck by its power and beauty, and the story of how the National Trust and many others work with this natural phenomenon to keep it … well, phenomenal.

## Keep this place special

Given that the Causeway has been around for aeons and will be around for aeons to come – albeit a bit more wind- and rain- and wave-lashed – it is right and important that we marvel at and care for it, that we learn from it and keep its environment as natural as possible. The Giant's Causeway and the elemental forces that caused it are bigger than all of us. Combined. But it's a joint effort that will keep such places of natural beauty special.

The staff and volunteers at the Giant's Causeway hope that all visitors are as moved by it as they are, and that you'll take something from this place – memories? a souvenir? a guidebook! – as well as renewed amazement at what Nature is capable of and the importance of doing what we can to look after her.